Presented to

On the occasion of

From

Date

© MCMXCVI by Barbour Publishing, Inc.

ISBN 1-57748-468-1

All Scripture quotations are taken from the Authorized King James Version of the Bible.

Published by Barbour Publishing, Inc., P.O. Box 719, Uhrichsville, Ohio 44683
http://www.barbourbooks.com

 Member of the
Evangelical Christian
Publishers Association

Printed in China.

Love Notes

BARBOUR
PUBLISHING, INC.

Many waters cannot quench love, neither can the floods drown it.

Song of Solomon 8:7

One word frees us of all the weight and pain in life. That word is love.

Sophocles

How do I love thee? Let me count the ways. . .If God choose, I shall but love thee better after death.

Elizabeth Barrett Browning

Love feels no burdens, thinks nothing of trouble, attempts what is above its strength, pleads no excuse of impossibility. It is therefore able to undertake all things, and it completes many things, and warrants them to take effect, where he who does not love would faint and lie down. Love is watchful and sleeping, slumbereth not. Though weary, it is not tired; though pressed, it is not straightened; though alarmed, it is not confounded; but, as a lively flame and burning torch, it forces its way upwards and securely passes all.

Thomas à Kempis

It is impossible to love and to be wise.

Francis Bacon

Do not keep the alabaster box of your love and friendship sealed up until your friends are dead. Fill their lives with sweetness. Speak approving, cheering words while their ears can hear them, and while their hearts can be thrilled and made happier. The kind things you mean to say when they are gone, say before they go.

George William Childs

My heart is like a singing bird
Whose nest is in a watered shoot;
My heart is like an apple tree
Whose boughs are bent with thickest fruit;
My heart is like a rainbow shell
That paddles in a halcyon sea;
My heart is gladder than all these
Because my love is come to me.

Christina Rossetti

A heart that loves is always young.

Greek proverb

And all for love, and nothing for reward.

Edmund Spenser

It is natural to love them that love us, but it is supernatural to love them that hate us.

Anonymous

Now what is love? I pray thee, tell.
It is that fountain and that well,
Where pleasure and repentance dwell.
It is perhaps that sauncing bell,
That tolls all in to heaven or hell:
And this is love, as I hear tell.

Sir Walter Raleigh

God gives us love. Something to love
He lends us; but, when love is grown
To ripeness, that on which it throve
Falls off, and love is left alone.

Alfred, Lord Tennyson

So sweet love seemed that April morn,
When first we kissed beside the thorn,
So strangely sweet, it was not strange
We thought that love could never change.
But I can tell—let truth be told—
That love will change in growing old;
Though day by day is nought to see,
So delicate his motions be.

Robert Bridges

Faults are thick where love is thin.

Anonymous

9

All other things, to their destruction draw,
Only our love hath no decay;
This, no tomorrow hath, nor yesterday,
Running it never runs from us away,
But truly keeps his first, last, everlasting day.

John Donne

~

Love knows hidden paths.

German proverb

~

There's a thing to remember; that you don't belong to yourself at all; and are bound to do the best you can with your time, and strength, and everything.

Grace Livingston Hill

There is no remedy for love but to love more.

Henry David Thoreau

How sweet the words of truth breathed from the lips of love.

James Beattie

We love him, because he first loved us.

1 John 4:19

At the touch of love everyone becomes a poet.

Plato

The heart has reason that reason does not understand.

Jacques Benigné Boussuet

But love's a malady without a cure.

John Dryden

No, the heart that truly loved never forgets,
But as truly loves on to the close,
As the sun-flower turns on her god, when he sets,
The same look which she turned when he rose.

Thomas Moore

Oh, life is a glorious cycle of song,
A medley of extemporanea;
And love is a thing that can never go wrong,
And I am Marie of Roumania.

Dorothy Parker

For all the law is fulfilled in one word, even in this; Thou shalt love thy neighbour as thyself.

Galatians 5:14

Love and a cough cannot be hid.

George Herbert

Love conquers all things: let us too give in to Love.

Virgil

My definition of marriage. . .it resembles a pair of shears, so joined that they cannot be separated; often moving in opposite directions, yet always punishing anyone who comes between them.

Sydney Smith

Love is the medicine of all moral evil. By it the world can be cured of sin.

Henry Ward Beecher

Love looks through a telescope; envy through a microscope.

Anonymous

On earth there is no heaven, but there are pieces of it.

Jules Renard

Flattery is from the teeth out. Sincere appreciation is from the heart out.

Dale Carnegie

He that falls in love with himself will have no rivals.

Benjamin Franklin

It is never loving that empties the heart, nor giving that empties the purse.

Anonymous

To love one maiden only, cleave to her,
And worship her by years of noble deeds,
Until they won her; for indeed I knew
Of no more subtle master under heaven
Than is the maiden passion for a maid,
Not only to keep down the base in man,
But to teach high thought, and amiable words
And courtliness, and the desire of fame,
And love of truth, and all that makes a man.

Alfred, Lord Tennyson

I court others in verse: but I love thee in prose: and they have my whimsies, but thou hast my heart.

Matthew Prior

And love's the noblest frailty of the mind.

John Dryden

Bid me to live, and I will live
Thy Protestant to be:
Or bid me love, and I will give
A loving heart to thee.

Robert Herrick

Now I know what Love is.

Virgil

Husbands, love your wives, even as Christ also loved the church, and gave himself for it.

Ephesians 5:25

And yet, by heaven, I think my love as rare
As any she belied with false compare.

William Shakespeare

Eternity is in love with the productions of time.

William Blake

If there be any truer measure of a man than by what he does, it must be by what he gives.

Robert South

Life may change, but it may fly not;
Hope may vanish, but can die not;
Truth be veiled, but still it burneth;
Love repulsed,—but it returneth!

Percy Bysshe Shelley

I loved not yet, yet I loved to love. . .I sought what I might love, in love with loving.

Saint Augustine

The supreme happiness of life is the conviction that we are loved.

Victor Hugo

Love built on beauty, soon as beauty, dies.

John Donne

To love is to place our happiness in the happiness of another.

Gottfried Wilhelm von Leibnitz

Love does not mean one thing in man and another in God. . . .The divine heart is human in its sympathies.

F. W. Robertson

Winter is on my head, but eternal spring is in my heart; I breathe at this hour the fragrance of the lilacs, the violets, and the roses, as at twenty years ago.

Victor Hugo

Faith is love taking the form of aspiration.

William Ellery Channing

If Music and sweet Poetry agree,
As they must needs (the Sister and the Brother)
Then must the love be great, 'twixt thee and me,
Because thou lov'st the one, and I the other.

Richard Barnfield

One may give without loving; but none can love without giving.

Anonymous

If thou must love me, let it be for naught
Except for love's sake only.

Elizabeth Barrett Browning

~

There is only one sort of love, but there are a thousand copies.

Francois de la Rochefoucauld

~

Nothing makes one feel so strong as a call for help.

George MacDonald

We are to add what we can to life, not to get what we can from it.

William Osler

LOVE. . .the golden key that opens the palace of eternity.

John Milton

Duty makes us do things well, but love makes us do them beautifully.

Anonymous

A "bit of Love" is the only bit that will put a bridle on the tongue.

Beck

Love does not consist in gazing at each other but in looking outward together in the same direction.

Antoine de Saint-Exupery

Love is more than gold or great riches.

John Lydgate

God loves each one of us, as if there was only one of us.

Saint Augustine

~

Then deem it not an idle thing
A pleasant word to speak;
The face you wear, the thought you bring
A heart may heal or break.

John Greenleaf Whittier

~

It is better to have loved and lost, than not to have loved at all.

Alfred, Lord Tennyson

He who cannot forgive others breaks the bridge over which he must pass himself.

George Herbert

He that loveth not knoweth not God; for God is love.

1 John 4:8

I knew it was love, and I felt it was glory.

Lord Byron

I never knew how to worship until I knew how to love.

Henry Ward Beecher

~

For in my mind, of all mankind
I love but you alone.

from The Nut Brown Maid

~

To love means to communicate to the other, that you will never fail him or let him down when he needs you, but that you will always be standing by with all the necessary encouragements. It is something one can communicate to another only if one has it.

Ashley Montagu

No cord nor cable can so forcibly draw, or hold so fast, as love can do with a twined thread.

Robert Burton

Better is a dinner of herbs where love is, than a stalled ox and hatred therewith.

Proverbs 15:17

What love is, if thou wouldst be taught,
Thy heart must teach alone—
Two souls with but a single thought,
Two hearts that beat as one.

Friedrich Halm

Love is like any other luxury. You have no right to it unless you can afford it.

Anthony Trollope

A man should never be ashamed to own he has been wrong, which is but saying in other words that he is wiser today than he was yesterday.

Alexander Pope

To love is to choose.

Joseph Roux

In peace, Love tunes the shepherd's reed;
In war, he mounts the warrior's steed;
In halls, in gay attire is seen;
In hamlets, dances on the green.
Love rules the court, the camp, the grove,
And men below, and saints above;
For love is heaven, and heaven is love.

Sir Walter Scott

Blessed is the influence of one true, loving human soul on another.

George Eliot

Love's like the measles, all the worse when it comes late.

Douglas Jerrold

So let us melt, and make no noise,
No tear—floods, nor sigh—tempests move,
'Twere profanation of our joys
To tell the laity our love.

John Donne

I ask thee for a thoughtful love,
Through constant watching wise,
To meet the glad with joyful smiles,
And to wipe the weeping eyes,
And a heart at leisure from itself,
To soothe and sympathize.

A. L. Waring

This is the final test of a gentleman: his respect for those who can be of no possible service to him.

William Lyon Phelps

The purest and most thoughtful minds are those which love colour the most.

John Ruskin

So let us love, dear Love, like as we ought,
Love is the lesson which the Lord us taught.

Edmund Spenser

We love being in love, that's the truth on't.

William Makepeace Thackeray

~

Love in a hut, with water and a crust,
Is—Love, forgive us!—cinders, ashes, dust;
Love in a palace is perhaps at last
More grievous torment than a hermit's fast.

John Keats

~

Those who have courage to love should have courage to suffer.

Anthony Trollope

Pains of love be sweeter far
Than all other pleasures are.

John Dryden

What do we live for if it is not to make life less difficult
for each other?

George Eliot

Love, thou art absolute sole Lord
Of life and death.

Richard Crashaw

When words refuse before the crowd
My Mary's name to give,
The muse in silence sings aloud:
And there my love will live.

John Clare

The speaking in perpetual hyperbole is comely in nothing
but love.

Francis Bacon

In the Spring a livelier iris changes on the burnish'd dove;
In the Spring a young man's fancy lightly turns to
thoughts of love.

Alfred, Lord Tennyson

37

There is no fear in love; but perfect love casteth out fear.

1 John 4:18

Stone walls do not a prison make
Nor iron bars a cage;
Minds innocent and quiet take
That for an hermitage;
If I have freedom in my love,
And in my soul am free;
Angels alone, that soar above,
Enjoy such liberty.

Richard Lovelace

The way to love anything is to realize that it might be lost.
Gilbert K. Chesterton

I will not let thee go.
Ends all our month-long love in this?
Can it be summed up so,
Quit in a single kiss?
I will not let thee go.

Robert Bridges

Like the sun, love radiates and warms into life all that it touches.

O. S. Marden

Money will buy a fine dog, but only love will make him wag his tail.

Anonymous

The question is not what a man can scorn, or disparage, or find fault with, but what he can love, and value, and appreciate.

John Ruskin

And walk in love, as Christ also hath loved us.

Ephesians 5:2